Ties that Bind

Ties that Bind

A Poetry Anthology by
The Bookoholics & Paper Towns

PAPER TOWNS
PUBLISHERS

PAPER TOWNS
PUBLISHERS

First published by
Papertowns Publishers
72, Vishwanath Dham Colony,
Niwaru Road, Jhotwara,
Jaipur, 302012

Ties that Bind

ISBN Print Book - 978-93-94670-10-5

Cover by Neha Agrawal
nehaa.2089@gmail.com

Editor's Note

"Friendships - and indeed most relationships - are measured in the closeness of hearts, minds and soul ties... not in the distance of physical miles or even the passing of time."

Rasheed Ogunlaru

In a world full of complex people, we choose who to be with. We choose who to let into out ever so little world, however detailed and disturbed, and this is what makes us who we are. While editing this book, there were a lot of poetries that made me realize how sensitive and utterly beautiful some ties are between two people, however they may be connected. Through blood, love, friendship, or distance. As long as there is comfort and an undeterred bond, the tie will always be special. This book holds a part of every writer that has contributed to it, and now it is yours. Truly and wholeheartedly. In hope that you keep it close and make good use of it in times of need. This special book is now yours.

- Shivang Ambardar

Contents

Ties that Bind

Akhilesh Sharma

Akhilesh Sharma, himself a passionate poet, is an ardent lover of Hindustani poetry and is greatly inspired by the masters such as Ghalib, Mir, Faiz, Iqbal and Gulzar. He belongs to Jammu and currently resides in Hyderabad. When he is not busy composing couplets, this 33 year old engineer works as a software professional in IT. While his poetry reflects his varied interests in art, literature, and history, he believes that a strong cup of coffee and a good book are the things that are worth living for.

ब्रेकअप

कहते हैं, रिश्ते तो गहने होते हैं,
लेकिन, गहने भी तो अक़्सर खो जाते हैं, टूट भी जाया करते हैं।

कुछ ऐसे ही संभाल कर रखा था इक रिश्ता,
गले से लगाया था किसी कीमती ज़ेवर कि तरहां,
पर करें क्या, इस दुनिया-ए-बाज़ार में,
जहां ज़ेवर अपनी कीमतों से अक़्सर गिर भी जाया करते हैं।

फासले तो घटते-बढ़ते रहते इन नौकरी की उलझनों में,
ये 'लौंग डिस्टेंस' के रिश्ते निभाने पड़ते हैं ऐसे कि,
कभी मैं आऊँ मिलने, और कभी तुम भी निकलो मुलाकात के लिए,
फिर भी इक डर है कि, बहुत ज़्यादा अगर घिस जाएं तो,
ये टूट कर बिखर भी जाया करते हैं।

ये लगता है कि सजावटी हों चुके हैं कुछ रिश्ते,
सिर्फ महफ़िलों कि चमक में जिन्हें निहारा जाता है,
और फिर 'चाभी-लौकरों' के अंधेरों में गिरफ्त रखा जाता है,
गर पुराने जब हो जाएं, तो लाकर नए गहने,
इन्हें भूल भी जाया करते हैं।

आज देखता हूँ कि वो जो गहना था तुम्हारे नाम का,
वो टूट गया है,
कोशिश तो की थी मैंने, लेकिन अब जोड़ नहीं सकता,
कि इसके कुछ हिस्से खो गए हैं,
ना वो चमक रही है अब, ना वो नयापन है,
घिस कर बस फीकी एक कड़ी सी रह गयी है,
कुछ रहा नहीं इसमें अब,
इसे 'ब्रेकअप' करते हैं।।

Akshara Narendran

A content writer by profession and an aspiring poet, Akshara has had articles published on topics related to Machine Leaning and Artificial Intelligence. A Delhi native, she is currently residing in a borough suitable to the workplace convenience.

Brown Bird

Sore wound marks still bleed when pressed hard.
With the courage of burning down the entire forest
and flooding the plains,
The brown bird fumed with fiery breath,
and her eyes swelled with burning tears.
The sky blared and discarded the blue comfort,
how to take a flight with wings tied.
Water, sky, air, rested under my wings;
once upon a time, the bird sighed.
Nectar of freedom and music of love made life worthwhile.
All in the past, the mighty demon glared,
while all the unseen fears started to cloud
the isle.
"Show your might, unleash valour,
let's get over the demon's pride", little flower
whispered.
Fire had swallowed the nest, the river boiled,
dried and then eventually died, while
the hopes lie tethered,
Bird looked at the hatched hidden new life,
an impending wait for a promising
tomorrow.
A tie that bound her to slavery,
a far-fetched dream of a free horizon, a painful truth
stuck in her throat, one she could never swallow.

Alisha Jain

Alisha is working as a Solutions Architect in an IT company in Hyderabad. Coding and reading books is something she is most passionate about. Recently, she has found her new love in putting out emotions through words and is determined to write and publish her own book someday, soon. You can connect with her on Instagram at @ajsepiphany where you will find her posting favourite books and quotes along with updates on her books.

I Am Just Like You

Chubby face, Radiant smile
My hysterical laughs, and the uncanny unibrow
Except my almond brown eyes
My looks, they say, are just like you.

I take risks and fear nothing
People find me intimidating
I am overwhelmed at the slight sight of one's misery.
My compassion, they say, is just like you.

I get angry and blabber
When I am hungry, I eat the entire platter
In the morning, I am a couch potato
At throwing silly PJs, I am a pro
My traits, they say, are just like you.
Munching late night
Or eating my favourite rajma rice.
I prefer extra chilies
And stay away from the sweet savories.
My tastebuds, they say, are just like you

I don't believe in superstitions and rituals,
but I have faith and I am spiritual
My beliefs, they say, are just like you

I read to enlighten.
I write to spread my perception.
I invest aggressively
And spend wisely.
My habits, they say, are just like you.

Like Father, Like Daughter
They say, I am just like you
But I never got to see you
I really wish God was not in need of you
So I could have seen how the way I am just like you, Papa.
My traits, they say, are just like you.

The Disconnected Connection

Every morning I wake up
I turn to your side and kiss your cheek
When I open my eyes to see you
I wake up from my dream

8months 5days since the breakup
A decade of relationship given up
All for the trifling pride
of the devout tribe
'Once in a lifetime Love' is deprived

When I am feeling low, and my life is hollow
When I am confound, or with pain bound
When I am irked, and need to crib
I think of you, replay your words to embitter
And I am filled with vigour

Be it festivals or birthdays
Anniversaries or any special days
You won't wish me, neither will I
Our lips will be sealed
But our hearts will give a silent cry
Wishing each other first, at the dead hour of night

We don't talk anymore, yet we speak volumes
Telepathy comes handy when gloom or in bloom
On a dark winter night, when the best of wool fails to keep
me warm
Our memories will bring the coziness and charm.

Not friends nor lovers, Not allies nor foes
Yet the fondness will remain, why, they will never know
They thought our separation will bring them honour
The fallacy deceived them, for Separation has made our bond stronger

Only in dreams we embrace and pour kisses
Futile are now all promises
Feelings have turned into poems, Conversations now exist in journal
This Disconnected Connection is our new normal.

Angel

Angel Srivastava is a poet and writer who found comfort in prose and grew up reading and breathing literature, which sparked her dream to become an author. After over a decade of writing for herself, and working as a professional content writer for magazines, websites and media houses, Angel has a uniquely composed voice, which cuts through the pages to reach your heart. When she isn't writing, she can be found with her muse and escape—cinema. Being inspired by stories, she hopes to inspire people to share their own. The intent that drives her work is to make the world a kinder place by making emotional expression the norm.

The Devil in the Details

When god created me,
He wrote me like a love letter.
Half drunk on stale alcohol,
And half, on the wild madness in his lover's eyes.
His hands, a little unsteady;
His eyes, red and tired.
He wrote me like a verse;
With unfinished sentences,
Still making sense.
Taking words from every love song ever written;
As if I was the muse of the bard himself.
He painted me like Van Gogh's Sunflowers;
Withering and blooming.
Knowing his masterpiece wouldn't be recognised;
Until, he shot himself.
An artist, so in love with his art;
That when god created me,
He poured himself in me,
Like his favourite brand of whiskey.
Glass after glass, as if on a bender.
He sculpted me from the ashes of
His day old cigarettes;
Mixed with a little rain water,
Making me smell of petrichor and menthol.
When god created me;
He did it on a weekend.
Because perfection cannot be hurried,
And the Devil is always in the details.

Aniruddha Hombali

Anuraddha is an author inspired by everyday life. He tries to reflect those unsung heroes and legends who touch our lives in a thousand small ways everyday, but, are mostly unrecognized for what they do. He likes to travel, read and indulge in good food.

Ties

The vales of the river,
The mounts of snow,
The plains of golden crops,
The mines of untold riches.

There are ties to them all,
They are in my heart,
They are a part of me,
They make me who I am.

The builders of magnificence,
The engineers of wonders,
The poets of old glory,
The artists of amazement.

They are my forebears,
They flow in my veins,
They are a part of me,
They make me who I am.

Where & When are these?
Who & What are they?
The best my blood has to offer,
The best my world has to offer.

These are my ties,
The ones I am bound to,
They are a part of me,
They make me who I am.

These ties are for us,
Not to bind us down,
But to let us soar,
To find new horizons.

Let me fly up & away,
Still tied like a kite,
They are a part of me,
They make me who I am.

Antarjot Kaur

Antarjot is a big dreamer by nature and tends to see the world through rose coloured glasses. She is a poet by heart and passionate for art and science, inquisitive, and creative. Also a lover of music and books, as they both are one of the things keeping her faith in the beauty of the world.

Sunlight, sunlight, sunlight

With sunlight on your face,
And tears slipping down your cheeks
I could see you falling with grace,
From the heavens above, right into my arms
Eyes like golden champagne,
bloody cheekbones, and freckles like stars
Under the sunlight, I see the crevices and
cracks upon your heart,
Oh, all the pain and suffering, the misery and melancholy
Give me, give me all of your pain
and I'll give you, give you,
the happiest moments of your life
I'll be your sun, and give you all of me
What can compare to the sunlight, sunlight, sunlight,
falling on your skin seeping into your soul, soul, soul
light breaks free out of every crack
as if you're the moon, and I'm the sun
Oh, I'll be your sun
and show you what the world is like
from the heavens above
and give you the happiest moments of your life
show you what love feels like
giving you all of my heart
Letting you feel the warmth of
Sunlight, sunlight, sunlight
Because I'll be your sun
And you'll be my moon.
I'll give you me
So that you can smile
living the happiest moments of your life.

Arohi Khedkar

Arohi pravin khedkar - is a 22 year old bibliophile, and does freelance book reviewing as an hobby. Quite recently, she has started to pen down her thoughts and feelings about every little thing she experiences in her life, and this poem is just one of them.

Missing Shadow

Under a shadow
She was growing till now
But all of a sudden
That's nowhere to be found.

The rage, the anger
Those suffocations and fear.
Surrounded by tons,
Yet no one feels dear.

She wants to grow,
And wants to feel.
And just like that somehow
She chose to heal.

There's a lot to prove
And a lot to learn
But all she can think of now
Is a burden which she can't bear.

There's always a ray of hope,
She has to gear up and shine
She can't just wait for the sun to shine bright
Or the moon to throw its light.

Now that she knew,
She has to overcome and fight.
Not just for herself but
For that Missing shadow of her life.

Arya Antherjanam V

Arya Antherjanam V is a researcher-turned-writer, who writes to get her inner chaos out. She has contributed to a couple of anthologies, and is a regular at spoken word poetry events. Her poems are a reflection of the world she engages with and the causes she wants to fight for.

For what binds us

No matter how many classics I read,
it's my fellow poets who make me want to
believe in the magic of breaking down the spell;
the ones who find escape in poetry, but not sure what from
the ones who write not to earn and live, but to fly and bleed
the ones who know that half of what they write is crap.
For what binds us is the vicious hunger for
the right words, the right dots, and the right pauses,
the ache in our hearts when the words
betray the aura of a comet passing by,
the struggle to live in the moment while
we leave them as a free verse.
For what binds us is the look on the face
of the words that do not make it to the poem,
the sour in our mouth when we gulp them down,
for not sounding too obvious,
for refraining from the menial,
the paranoia of reader's eyes grazing between the lines,
digging up the heart we buried beneath the most boring vowel;
the quest for the seventh Horcrux ending at the grave.

For what binds us is the pulse speeding up
at the thought of a thief barging into our head,
looting us of all the words, putting them
exactly the way we wanted,
calling it their poem,
not knowing whether to be terrified or proud of it.
That one day we wake up and no stars
plummet from the eyes of a lover we lost,
no clock in the room shows tok before tik,
no crevices on the palm are devoid of obsolete redness, and
the poem looks like a sunset we can never go back to.

Astha Anand

Astha Anand is the author of 2 published poetry and quotes books, part of multiple anthologies, and onto her next book. She believes in expression through art, and is an avid reader, home cook, and a dreamer for most part of life. She is also a technical consultant by the day. As a warm human being and lover of conversations, you are sure to come across the writer if you spend a couple of minutes in an intriguing conversation with her. Currently, she shares her work on Instagram at soulfood189.

Soulmates of a Different Kind

It will happen again, you know.
In the next lifetime,
And the ones that'd follow,
When we lock eyes for the first time,
And a million other times after,
Trying to understand,
Where our story fits in this chapter.

What is that we feel,
The pull, the familiarity,
Why do we seem to know each other,
With this unclear, clarity.

We would know the outcome,
I'd never be yours,
Neither you mine,
But to keep us together,
These stars align.

There is a part of our souls
That we will always share,
A history, some glances,
Some moments to bare,
Which will keep us in each other's path,
Crossing every time,
Not knowing you too well,
But well enough to rhyme,

And wondering why even though it isn't,
This seems like a bluff,
Our story built on 'maybe' and 'what ifs'
Honestly, would be just enough.

Ayesha Khalid

For Ayesha, the journey of art and language is always like an untravelled road. Being a geography enthusiast, art is like a pole star. She fails and she learns. So, with hope in her heart, she weaves alphabets bracketed to each one of us to spread light, happiness, and honesty.

Words

words are like
diet food
if the ratio is imbalanced
it will disturb the whole routine,
words are like
prices of petrol and diesel
if the hike is high
it will make the proletarian cry,
so your words should have errors
low when you pronounce your
concerning speech,
speech that glimmers like
fairy lights, making the room
of your heart bright with
colors of aurora lights.

once in a blue moon
when all the flowers of the
the same garden bloomed
in the same season
to celebrate an occasion,
the roots used to regenerate
which our oldsters implanted,
those roots were ancient ethical tales
which was unfolded in front of us
by Nana Jaan, which are still close to our hearts,
those stories took a u-turn
to build a safe space in our home again.

the way he untangled all the
nuts and bolts of the word "word"
it was spread in layers on the
canvas of our mind, those teachings
felt so warm
artistic, and ethereal
and was brimmed with
a new charm.

that day, it was a
relatively warm and pleasant noon.
'we were called lazy sloths'
as we booked nana jaan's side for
our daily show,
"his stories are made in heaven"
as soon as he head started
the essence of petrichor used to
embrace our soul,
and the storyteller was on
stage to teach us lessons
taking those colorful hues
as a subject or say attention.

"your words should be like a rainbow"

entwined with hues of
blessing and shades of love
so that when a stroke of that shade
is perceived by someone's ears
it tranquilizes the soul
like prayers do,
it should be musical in nature
like the sound of a flute
having poetic and humming gestures.

he said,
your words should heal the broken soul
and not be the part of any stupid troll
your words should be weaved with
love of your mother's speech
not any oxymoron preach.

grandpa's lessons were profound
and intriguing like warm lullabies

he said-
your dictionary of words should
always fire the bullets of delicacy
and allegiance
rather than disintegrity and cunningness
so that your heart will also be unbounded from
viciousness.

Ayush Amlan

He is not just Ayush Amlan,
But his Goddess' plan,
Given a new life by the blessing of his parents,
Nineteen years back,
And trying to be one of those daring aspirants,
Who never fears to pave their own track...

Flap

Flap your wings and fly away,
Until yet another day,
After going around the world,
And spreading the worth of your word,
You will flap in the reverse direction,
And return for my affection,
I will feed,
So that you once again sweat and bleed,
Without any greed,
For those in and beyond your breed,
You ought to take the lead,
You may dare to delete,
The memory of my contributions for you,
But never desire to be freed,
From global responsibilities on you,
Fly for an independence blessed with wisdom,
Not for the conceit of extra freedom,
Because you flap your wings in the biosphere,
That belongs to our sphere,
The world shall give you immense pleasure,
And openly offer its treasure,
But remember the art of mutualism,
Else you will become the paragon of parasitism,
Still justifying it to be commensalism,
But why justify?
Dare to rectify,
Else your social identity shall nullify,
Because you may forget me,
But never forget the world that allowed you to be free,

Because I will silently accept your ignorance,
But the world shall reply with abhorrence,
So the next time you flap your wings,
To see what your flight brings,
This mother expects nothing,
But be it autumn or spring,
Never refuse to serve the world,
That gave love to the purpose of your word...

Ayushi Gupta

Ayushi is a girl trying to salvage her heart by writing, hoping to bring a change in someone's life.

Like a Leaf

Does love actually fade?
Like the autumn dried leaf
Separated from its tree
Swayed into the air
Until it is nothing
Until it fades away
Into nothingness.
Does love fade like that?
Or it still remains there
Dried up somewhere
Like that dried up leaf
A part of it still left behind
Or a part of it still abandoned somewhere
Waiting to be crunched upon
Maybe love still stays there
Waiting to be crunched upon
Just like that leaf.

Bhargab Das

Bhargab Das is a daydreamer who lost his interest in reality. He keeps trekking into his own fictional land named HEBJ in search of poetry and prose this world has not heard of. With a sarcophagus mind, the personification of science in philosophy is his main motive to exist.

Chaismus of Birth and Renaissance

Her scintillating grey hair, once silk black flock;
But it still smells the same.
Gratitude, the youth still shines on her exquisite smile.
"Learn to cook yourself before we leave.", She often mocks
now. Heart aching yet she reflects the truth of nature.
'Stop, you are not going anywhere', a self-consolidation.

Now, a retired personnel,
He discovered his culinary talents, "Better late than never",
he preaches. The fingers that I used to hold upon as we
always walked out
Now grabs my hand as I help him to get up from his rocking
chair. The once proud moustache has not lost its charms yet.
"I have lived my part of life, now it's your turn, young man."
He pets me on my shoulder as I bring him his medicines.

The Archetype, I grew up following their footsteps.
Even their omnipotent corporeal way of disciplining the child
within me ould only be deciphered in the language of love.
And now as I established myself with a career, they bless me:
"Live your life as if every moment is a last one".
I imitate this lesson as a mockery rather than blessings since
I, Drenched in enigma,
Exoculated by exacerbating agony,
Can not bear their rapid aging.

They blessed me with my youth while themselves turned
pale and grey. The recognitions and accolades hanging
on the wall that I have earned, They say are unparalleled
acknowledgements of their successful parenting. Maybe,
since all these names mean nothing to me,

Without them in my life.
It's this auroma of their presence that makes this house a home.
It's this laughter that fuels the hearth and keeps us warm.
It's this voice that soothes any sheer despondence inside.

"Dinner's ready", my exuberant mother's boisterous summon
Now left as a reverberating echo within the borders of this
apathetic house. Reminiscing which leads to renaissance of
our broken souls:
Renaissance of the subtle smile that once she taught us to.

Brahmani Nandigam

Brahmani has been a quiet child since childhood and has always found comfort in between the pages. When she learnt that speaking can never suffice to express how deep her thoughts run, she chose poetry to show the world, how she has been seeing it.

To the flower that she has been

To the flower that she has been.

Has she known?
Has she ever known how brave she has been
For choosing to remain the delicate petals that she were
Though continuously aware of the thorns she was being surrounded by?

Has she known?
Has she known how selfless she has been
For spreading all those exquisite fragrances
Despite knowing that she is going to wilt one day?

Has she known?
Has she known how loving she has been
For giving all that she has
And expecting nothing but their happiness in return?

Has she known what a wonder she has been?
Has she known how magical her presence is?
Has she known how much of a difference she brings into the world just by existing?
Has she known?
I wonder if she does!

Chetana Kamath

Chetana appreciates the simple things in life. She strives to work towards her goals and puts her heart and soul into her work. She is an avid reader and dreams of owning a house full of bookshelves. A girl of a few words, she believes that her work speaks for herself. She resides in the beautiful coastal city of Mangalore in Karnataka, India.

Walk with Me

Walk with me,
For you are my sunlight
On a rainy day.
Walk with me,
For you are my moon
Watching over me
As I sleep peacefully.
Walk with me,
For you are my beacon
On a stormy night.
Walk with me,
For you are my rainbow
In a world of blacks and greys.
Walk with me,
For you are my blanket
On days cold and harsh.
Walk with me,
For you are the hero
In my little story.
Walk with me,
For you are a book
To guide me forever.
Walk with me,
For you are the lemon
In my lemonade.
Walk with me,
For you are a song
In my favourite playlist.
Walk with me,
For you are my best friend
And no one can change that.

Devin Aceton

Poetry, for Devin, is the reason he feels that he can be heard without actually speaking. That he can be acknowledged for his skill, that he can be free in a world he created. It's far from peaceful, but it brings him peace. It is his escape to a place where nothing can hurt him.

Wings

That numb feeling,
Void of all emotions,
I look up at the starry night,
With the lack of exhilaration.

Ears all around the place,
The pretense of obliviousness
Their words carved onto my soul,
Not knowing, I heard everything they said.

I was alone in a busy world,
Mentally ill, I was made out to be
A freak of nature, unfit of their construct,
No one cared to hear out my plea.

I felt tainted,
Their disgust rubbing off on me
The satisfaction to pursue my heart's content,
Slowly whittling down my skin.

Did I not deserve happiness…
Or the chance to chase it?
Or should I turn into one of those,
Who has eyes, but still can't see?

Misconceptions spread,
A patient; That's all they could see.
Having enough of everything,
I let my voice run free.

Deafening silence, my heart disarray,
My steps quick, scurrying away.
The warm feeling churning in my heart,
The smile never wandered off.

Pushed down by commoners,
Amidst their nonsensical logic,
Yet my stand strong, my voice stronger,
I let them hear, be raged even,
That their norm will never ensnare my will,
And that will be my victory.

Quashed under their binaries,
I rose like a phoenix from ash,
Nearly coercived in their delusions,
But karma says; what you do, will always get you back.

And I ain't that patient, to begin with…

Dhruv Malpani

Dhruv Malpani is 18 years old and is currently in first year of his law school. His favourite author is William Shakespeare, and he considers him his inspiration to Writing. Other than Writing and Reading Literature, his other interests include Law, Psychology, History, Philosophy and Archaeology.

Shackles

A helpless soul he was
Suffocated by the torments of the world.

Some things he said in words
But much in his heart remained unsaid.

Years of torture inculcated patience in him, but they also made him forget
What emotions were,

He saw himself as yet another drop of existence,
in this vastness of the ocean waters.

Fathoms deep down his soul, he was no more not dead
And there was no going back .. He was sure.

He was alone
But it didn't bother him much before,
His loved ones had abandoned him At least then, he had himself
But now he lost himself too.

The world taught him to put on a happy face
But nobody cared to tell him
About the chaos that is being created within.

He would be so lost in his thoughts at times
That he'd even forget what he was reckoning about, in the first place.

He gave up trying to break off from the chains that he had built for years now.

He was trapped in the walls he designed ad infinitum.

He was enslaved by his own negative musings
He was paused in his own imagination,
While the world moved forward.

He locked himself in a completely lightless room, waiting to die,
To die, to dream yet again in his sleep of death.

He started laughing out loud
As his last few breaths drew away from him.

His laughter turned into tears of salvation and as his conscience grew,
He knew he didn't fear the arrival of death . He only feared the awakening into life.

But if he catered to that fear,
Then he would be no better than the rest of the world,
And hence, he decided to overcome that fear and encounter it for the first time in his life.

So, he slowly stood up
Taking in the fresh air, breathing his first, undoing his act of entrapment,
Coming out of his imaginative world , letting go of all the negativity.

And finally, started living for the first time with a new perspective towards life.

Dipen Dave

Dipen would love to be called a Writer and a Reader someday but they are slowly and steadily in progress. Those two are the inseparable part of his life; he writes to make sense of the nonsense in the world and reads for the very same reason. He believes in strongly raising his opinions and spreading a message through his words that would resonate. To sum it up, he is just a human trying to spread humanness in little ways.

Three on a Bench Theory

Summary: The poem is about a theory that I keep as a self-inspiration. The theory of three on a bench summarizes that you'll always be happier or sadder than others at all times. This case applies to each and everyone and we have to acknowledge the existence of that fact and not be burdened by it, only then we'll be able to be peaceful and content.

I am just a human,
Just a human like you,
that knows one thing
that our feeling's few

All constant comparison
All automatic assumption
All overly overthinkers
All sorrowed sinkers
That one constant tick
That tick in mind,
why aren't we happy,
and why nothing's ever fine,
why me, why me, always me?
happiness in no sight.
What will I do?
and when will I fight?

About this I had to do something,
or anything
but just not nothing
Then I analyze,
Overthink
Evaluate and Scrutinize

I took a paper, a paper and pen
I wrote down a theory, a theory of three on a bench
In left of me there's a man
That man has hands stuck on his head
He is less happy, less rich and less witty than me
He has some troubles
That are quite bigger than mine
But when I sit next to him
I feel I am quite fine

and then there's one right to me
The man has arms folded and smile so bright
He's happy and fulfilled and seems to party all night
He is more jolly, more wealthy and more clever than me
He has some troubles
That might be smaller than mine
When I sit next to him
I feel I am quite "not" fine

But I made peace with the fact
A fact that there will always be a comparative
On left as well as right
And even if I'll be whatsoever in this world
My name would be shouted and heard
I'll always be the one,
The one with someone on left, and on right
But I'll adjust myself in the middle
For me, For you, For all of you,
There will always be a right and always a left
You be the middle, and go for that quest
You be the middle, and still go for that quest

Garima Jain

Every time Garima looks at the world, she wants to write about it. It may be in the form of short poems or prose, but she wants her views to reach everyone.. May her words help you see the world in a different light.

A Reminder

Reminder for all the souls who are fighting a battle everyday
Reminder for all the souls who are tired of this struggle everyday
I know it's taking a lot of time
I know it's feeling like a lost battle
but how will you answer your reflection
who will ask you why you left your ground in the battle
You have no one answerable but yourself
You have no excuses to pass on the blame but yourself

Gayathri Ramkumar

Gayathri Ramkumar is full of fun and enthusiasm. She is living life to the fullest in the southern part of India. She talks about motivation and building passion. When not writing, she can be found reading YA fiction and meandering into the flow of thoughts with the fictional characters.

Destiny

From sharing memes to sharing hearts,
Sure, 'twas a roller coaster of emotions.
Stares to smiles to words to time,
Thought it was always mine.
Despite spelling those beautiful words,
Plans were made, after the destiny's swords.
Hoped she would stay and things are on our way, until it's time for the destiny to take us far away.
Letting the rest of our lives in profound surprise :)

To the World of my Dreams

For the umpteenth time, I hear you solace
my soul in despair.

"I swear not to scare, but to constantly care for the priceless bond we share.

Deciding to live the real, in surreal,
rewinding the reminiscent solidarity and the ties that lived in proximity.
All I wish is promising to tear
the distance and dare
to face the fate and declare our destiny.

By imploring the universe to let you - 'the Ideal human soul' as 'the tie'
that binds my life!" :)

Ishita Mehal

Ishita is a reader who also writes passionately about her feelings and half-baked observations of the world around her, while petting four kittens, her only friends. Being a cinephile, she loves dissecting, analyzing and discussing about almost every other movie and series. Lastly, politics is something she is interested in and follows, given the dark drama it entails.

A Raging Storm

A silent night, a sense of calm,
No movement besides the whistling of wind or rustling of leaves,
Aching feeling about a sinner doing harm
And a threatening storm causing thousands to grieve.

A mute spectator, a complicit in crime,
Witnessed a deadly massacre without speaking up
For fellow humans, more similar to us than different, who didn't align
With the sinners in power enjoying in the rich club.

In the face of ugliness and fascism and hate,
None awakened to pacify this raging storm.
Naive to assume they're guarded behind the segregating gates,
They chose to easily conform instead of calling for reform.

A vanishing pride, a looming shame,
The land I thought was mine but belonged to all,
Is slowly burning into ashes by the communal flames,
Is breaking into smithereens, descending towards a tragic fall.

A ticking clock, a sign of time passing by,
Before using the power to elect, introspect and reflect,
Perhaps better sense of mind will prevail that'll always ask why
And will speak up, will stand up for fellow humans with whom we inextricably interconnect.

Jaithun Bi J

Jaithun Bi is a striving content creator (Youtuber and Instagram blogger), writer and final year zoology student (UG) from Chennai. She graduated from women2women virtual University.

She runs her own podcast show, "RISE ABOVE WITH JAITHUN BI", and it's doing pretty well. 45% of her listeners are from India, 41% are from the USA, and others are from other countries. People show their love towards each episode where she talks about climate change, productivity, the environment, women empowerment, and more.

She has also co-authored 3 different poetry anthologies.

She is also the recipient of the Global Extraordinary Women Award for 2022.

She always says, "Make love and peace contagious. Let's learn together and rise together."

Tragical Romance

Fallen in love with me poetically in a library
Lying under the moon and dreaming of the time when we will marry
He loves to make a love playlist
Walking with hands tied together on city roads in white mist

Someone whose kindred spirit is nature
Someone who fancies my poems and makes me feel safer
Someone who adores summer more than winter
Someone who pinky swears and takes dramatic oaths
Someone who is not a fan of socializing and greatly opposes it

A crack in me
And he is the light that gets in me

I'm fowled and flawed
But he loves me with them beyond
He doesn't come to fix me
He is the keeper of my heart's key

His laugh became my favourite sound
And we used to vibe to our song on the radio on the ground

I ran barefoot down the hallway of an abandoned castle
How great it will be to get together and travel

But at last, I wanted him to let go of me
Tragical Romance and all is what I see
I just wanted to live with him in my memories
Because after all
Everything was a maze of thoughts and malleable memories

Wrote a letter to him
To Dear soulmate
With all my love,
The unrequited love of your life

I will be waiting to meet him
I hope one day!
Maybe one day!
Maybe one fine day!

Jinali Chawda

Jinali is 22 and lives six feet under the books. She is mostly about Taylor Swift and is a little too much into characters made up of ink. Writing has been an escape for her since 2013, and currently, she is trying her hand in blogging, getting her work published, and hopes to get more of her work published in the future.

Reflections

When I have you lying next to me
Hand in hand, staring at the empty ceiling
I have nothing on my mind but you,
It is at that moment, I call you 'mine'

I hold you close, I hold you tight
But you slip away every time
Like the water, I hold in my hand
It is at that moment, I realize the 'pain'

How funny is the idea of 'US'?
I hold you when I know, you think of her
I wish to be united when I know, reflections never do
Do you see it, too? We are right beside and yet miles apart,
Like the sea and the sky
Like the soul and the body
Like the light and the shadow
We go hand in hand but never close.

How wretched is the idea of 'ending'
Like the death separates the soul from the heart
Like the tears that rolled down our cheeks
And we smile when deep inside there is just grief
We found the soulmate when our souls belong to someone else
We are the reflection, you and I
A part of each other but looking for ourselves somewhere else.

Kajal Kumari

Kajal Kumari is a graduate student from Jamshedpur. She is a temporary writer in fiction on Wattpad. She indulges herself in reading classical, fictional, and self-help books. She has a positive attitude towards her life.

Emotion

This poem is dedicated to the memory of my brother. I hope the readers can relate to their dear ones.

While sitting under the starry night,
And looking at the moon so bright,

I lay there thinking about life,
And the rat race outside which I have to strive.

Feeling like an incompetent in the world full of competition,
But then, bethinks me of a man who is always there to clear
my vision.

Perseverance, passion, commitment was all that he demanded,
Clearing my self-doubt, a helping hand he expanded.

Mahak Sonkar

Mahak Sonkar is an emerging young poet. Born and raised in Varanasi, she is pursuing MBBS from King George's Medical University, Lucknow, India.

Her first composition got published in the poetry anthology, Heavy Lies The Crown published by PaperTowns India and marketed by The Bookholics, at the age of nineteen.

Currently residing in Lucknow, she holds a record in short stories/poetry compositions and a couple of commendable achievements in the All India Essay Writing Competitions.

Besides, she's a great fan of Sherlock Holmes and holds an eternal love for music.

Reach her @the_mahak & @thedarkliners on Instagram.

Let me Be Your Glitter

You're that serenity,
Who understood my maturity..
You stayed always calm,
In my every dusk & dawn..
You laughed at my jokes,
And made me survive every stroke..
You collected my tears,
And made me overcome all my fears..
Maybe you're a blessing,
Maybe you're an angel..
I don't know your origin,
But, I known your descending..
You're my gold, you're my glitter,
Trust me you're beautiful & rare..
If you ever have a doubt,
Just see yourself through my eyes...

Malika Rani

Working her way amidst the chaos of life, Malika is always up for a laugh, cry, and everything in between.

I am Sorry

This poem describes the relationship that we share with ourselves. The compassion, love and forgiveness that we need to give ourselves and try to let go of being our own enemy.

How many times have you told this?
To a friend
To a foe
To a Jane and John Doe
To a passerby on the street
Running into you on purpose
You know where he was going, didn't you?
Yet you said I'm sorry
I'm sorry that your hand was on my chest
My chest should have been empty
My lips should've been shut
So you didn't have to slip me that drink
My waist should've been smaller
For your self-esteem to not sink
My mind should have been clearer
I'm sorry to burden you with my thoughts
I am a regretful oversharer
Even though you are a merciless flame bearer
I am sorry
I take too much space
Lie on your face
That I am comfortable with your pace
I'm sorry.
That I am uncomfortable with your pace
Yes,
I'm talking to you
I'm sorry I don't give you enough credit

I blame you for another's fault
You stay in bed all day from the panic
And I brush it off saying it's just meaningless manic
I tear off your worth
By bleeding your skin
I punish you
For no unholy sin
You're more than I thought you were
I'm less than you'll ever be.
I'm sorry, you.
I'm sorry, me.

Niharika Hayat

Niharika is a banker by profession who loves to read books. Growing up, fascinated by books, she started to have an interest in penning down her thoughts. Later, she realised she can write and that's how she started writing, and absolutely fell in love with it. An old school at heart, she loves to sketch, listen to retro music and explore different genres of poetry and books.

सुकून का कोना

मैं न जब भी घर जाती हूँ
तो जो मेरी अलमारी में किताबें रखी हैं
उन्हें देखने का मन होता है हर बार
जैसे हम किसी का हाल चाल पूछते हैं न
कई महिनों बाद, ठीक वैसे ही
उस अलमारी को जब भी खोलूं
तो लगता है अपनी दुनिया में आ गई हूँ
ज़मीन पे बैठ जाती हूँ और
एक एक करके उन्हें खोलती हूँ
वहीं रख देती हूं अपने आस पास
और देखती रहती हूँ
जैसे कोई माँ अपने बच्चे को
सोता हुआ देख कर खुश होती है
ठीक वैसे ही..
इनके बिना अब.. मुश्किल सा लगता
इनकी आदत है मुझे अब..

Pranita Kalekar Savale

Pranita Kalekar Savale obtained a Bachelor's Degree in Engineering.

Poetry is her passion, energy and in true sense it gives her feeling of satisfaction that she is in touch with people through her words of poetry. Her poetry comes from certain incidences and observing people around her.

Grandma

I am very keen to listen when she speaks
Every word that comes out of her mouth is not just a thing..It means everything..
In reality, it's a true blessing…
Her small eyes within those wrinkles
When you look at them, they always shine and twinkle...
Always a smiley face
Who is full of grace..
Who always chooses to be simple
Who has a cute little dimple..
She is full of patience and persistence
She is always a happy soul
She knows more to give than to take
She is really a cherry on the cake
When I make funny faces, she laughs out loud
When I think of her I feel proud..
The moment we come to know love is found rare
The selfless soul who always cares...
When we have a grandmother who is so caring
Ultimately, we will come to know who is the most lovely human being…
I am the luckiest one to have a grandmother like her…
Although she is not here, I can feel her..
Each and every day I really miss her…
Moments which we spent together might be few..
But they are far more to rewind, remind, recollect and relive…

Prarthana Guha

A doctoral student by day and a writer at night, Archrista(pen name) has always had a passion for exploring different genres of literature. Short poetries to novels - the world of words has grown inside her through time. She regularly writes on online platforms like Wattpad and NbliK, and dreams of publishing her own novel someday.

For You

They asked me to wear a flower crown.
I looked pretty.
They asked me to walk as soft as morning breeze.
I looked gentle.
They asked me for the voice of a quiet river.
I looked calm.
I waited.
The 'me' was nowhere to be found.
Lost.
Lies grew in me.
Small, then huge.
Until one ordinary sunset brought you to me.
All naked and raw.
Dented and crooked.
I knew.
I wasn't afraid to show my thorns anymore.
I didn't try to hide the storm anymore.
I never forgot to embrace the chaos anymore.
I saw.
I saw the image in the mirror, wild and true.

Stay, Mate

You show me a thousand reasons to leave.
I will show you one reason to stay.
Hold me, mate.
Put your worries away.
Hold onto that one reason, if you may.
Promise me, mate.
On days of pale, grey and blue
You reach me and I hold you.
Save the pain, mate.
Destiny will see to your pain.
It was always us together, so we'll be again.

Prince Gautam

Born in the small town of Baripada, Odisha, Prince has lived in metropolitan cities like Jamshedpur and Bhubaneswar as well as small towns like Dangoaposi and Baripada. This gave him the exposure of the society which later converted into the passion to know about people and their livelihood. Writing started out as a hobby from the early years of his life, and he was always fascinated with horror and psychological novels, stories, and essays that speak about a concept that is larger than life.

Over the course of time, he got busy with his career but later he decided not to stop writing, keeping the storyteller in him alive, and gradually crafting the art to reach the genuine audience. Author of three books (You Seem Depressed!?!!/ Father- A Short Story/ Blues & Butterflies- Volume I), he has worked on many fiction books which he will gradually release over time.

A Fascinating Journey of an Abstract Minded Girl

She drew mountains
with crayons.
She expressed her heart
through paper.
She craved for
Crackers
some samosas and wafers.
She watches her classmates,
they always look cheerful.
They always celebrate.
There was none
with whom she can be friends.
No one has even a single quality that befits her personality,
there was nobody with whom she resonates.

Her mother was a maid,
her father lost his legs.
He met an accident,
just about a couple of years back.
Though they were poor
her mother taught her not to fear.
Being brave is not just an option,
it was a necessity,
in this world full of toxins.
You cannot cure everyone,
but you can become your own vaccine.
In a world full of humans,
you need to work more efficiently than machines.

Tough words from a tough lady
made her strong and rock steady.
She was not good at maths, science or language.
Her reading skills were average.
Being poor might be leverage,
but she got the courage
to overcome obstacles
and to prove wrong to all those spectators
who mock and laugh at her.
They try to choke her and treat her like amateurs.

A connoisseur
recognized talent in her.
The magic she created on paper
For her, it was a gallant piece of artwork.

She is a painter now.
She visited fifty countries.
She made her parents proud.
She doesn't like wafers anymore,
She has found love for the pastries.

This is her journey,
That I abstractly conclude.

Priti Bapat Deshpande

Priti was born in Thane, Mumbai. Growing up, she developed an avid interest in Reading and Writing.

She believes writing poetry is a shortcut from heart to heart. Apart from writing poems; paintings and music keep her busy. Being a bookworm and deep thinker, she enjoys her own company.

Priti believes that she doesn't need a reason to be happy, although she smiles more when left to her own devices.

You can connect with her on Instagram @poetry.priti

Love

Early chilly dawn
spreading rays of crimson red,
both hunters patiently
waited under the shade.

When the flock of geese
flew over hunter's head,
sound of quackling turned
to bang bang instead.

Some straight down
while others safe ahead,
A hen from the pair
dropped down amongst the dead.

Her partner came back
did not want to be parted,
crying, circling from above
never left, though afraid.

'Be quick and take a shot'
an experienced hunter guided,
Bang! Again goes the gun
and nothing more needs to be said.

Good winter sport for hunters
and lover's tragic end!!!

Priyanka Bhutani

Priyanka is a keen observer and passionately loves to devote her time to reading and writing. She started writing at an early age, but her writings were typically confined to papers only. One day, while reading her friend's blog, she also realized to present her writings to everyone. So, on the same day, the world came to know about the writer behind a shy girl.

She always tries to learn from others' experiences also because that empowers her to have more clarity in thoughts and in living an exuberant life.

"Indeed, expressing gratitude and apologizing are the sacred ties that bind!"

Ties that Bind

Do you know what are the ties that bind us?
Don't worry, dear, we'll soon discuss!

When I go through something I can't explain
You refuse to sleep and ignore your back pain!
Maa, you are the only one who keeps on checking me over and again.

Yes, Maa, love and care are the ties that bind us,
And because of that I hardly fuss!

Though I've not done much to make you proud
But one day I will for sure, I vowed!
Papa, you are the only one who always pushes me to stand out of the crowd.

Yes, Papa, strength and belief are the ties that bind us,
And you keep on motivating me till I board the bus!

After rushing all day here and there
I cry out tears of joy with your genuine care!
Bhai, you are the only one who's there in the darksome night of despair.

Yes, Bhai, trust and understanding are the ties that bind us,
And when I don't smile you keep on saying, "Daa, let's discuss!"

Priyanka Mishra

I'm a literature student. Finding love, art and peace through words. You can find my poems on WordPress at: https://echoingsoul209210811.wordpress.com/

Musings of Love

I'm writing

A beautiful tale today

A tale of love

A musing between lovers.
Our hearts are pieces

Which gets mended when together

And destroyed with absence of other.

I just pour down every little word

And when its for you,

They become poem

Without any due.
I've got words

You make them feelings

I have scars

You kiss them with love that unravels

When emotions decipher

Your presence is what I crave for

And when I had ruins

You became my home,

The pleasant peace I wasn't aware of.
This longing won't get buried

Untill you come and kiss away all worry.

Purvasha Nath

Student at Parul University, Purvasha loves to read and write. Imagination is what makes her write.

Rainy Eve

Peter pater rain drops arriving at the
window corner,
me hurrying to grab the dry clothes
where your sight met mine for the first
time.
Me breathing heavily seeing the water
drops passing through your body
and you watching me as the slanting
lines before me clapping the earth.
Those few moments of intimacy
touched our hearts, ofcourse knowing
we'll never meet again.

Riddhi Bhargava

A teen bookish nerd who writes poetry (and attempts to write novels!) in her free time, Riddhi runs a book blog over on WordPress, since books are her first love! When not reading, you can find her baking, bingeing Netflix, watching cricket, listening to Taylor Swift, Why Don't We, or some other cool pop artist. Besides reading and blogging, music, coffee, chocolates and dogs are her primary sources of happiness.

Tied

I felt at peace
Because you were gone
I felt blissful
Because you were gone.

The house was silent
I wasn't in constant fear
Of what you would do
Should I take a single misstep.

I wasn't in constant agony
Since you weren't there
To taunt me
Should I take a single misstep.

I wasn't in constant pressure
To be at my best
I could actually breathe
Even if it was just for a moment.

But tomorrow you return
And I will no longer be free
I'll be tied to our responsibilities
I'll be suffocated by them.

I wanted to be free
Of all the ties that bound us.
I wanted to the bird that flew free
Not the one sitting meekly in a cage.

Rupali Muley

Rupali is a developer by profession and dreamer by heart, loves to read and write. She is found mostly humming, scribbling and giggling around. Her love for books and words, started ageing just like the old fine wine, allowed her to publish 2 books 'Something from Somewhere, and 'Archived', of her own.

Constantly thinking of changing the world, just by her words, and holding a museum of memories of her loved ones close to her heart.

Come, take me there

And then, he went there, to that same place,
of nothingness, where everyone wanted to go.
The place where all the books were kept,
where all characters reside,
And weave beautiful stories.
And then, just like other love stories,
They started meeting each other
In that same place,
Where everyone wanted to weave stories and even live them.
The day was Monday, of old December withering the leaves of trees and leaving the skies and tress, gloomy and grim, and just like all other days,
He went there, and sat there
At his daily corner,
Started reading her between the lines,
By hearing, whatever unspoken she has
By saying, whatever unheard she has,
By hugging her tight, so as to hear her heart
Beating and absorbing those beats himself, so much to allow his heart to beat in sync of hers.
Well, I've always heard that, that place is not good,
You'll go in search of something,
You'll keep on watching something else, you'll catch hold of something, and you'll bring home something else.
But still, he was truly in love with her
What if, she was not a mere reality
What if, she never belonged to the real world,
What if, she was an imagination
Cleared the clouds of his thoughts,
And wiped the uncertain fear away,

Yes, I was wrong, he belonged to her
and she belonged to that place
She was his choice, and he,
He loved his choice,
What if, she's just a character in the book
What if, she's just a combination
Of someone's imagination and muse, she was the poetry
embedded in the pages of his heart,
And he, he was seeker of a poem,
In the world of hearts beating
In a sync of symphony
Somewhere in between, dream and reality
Somewhere in between, fiction and poetry
After reading, he closed the book,
Looked up and smiled, to the nothingness leaving that place,
he looked back and smiled,
Seeing his love peeping from the glass window,
Where all the books were kept,
Where all the characters reside,
And weave beautiful stories,
He took a last glance at his favorite muse,
Residing in his favorite book
Closing his eyes, and spoke to himself 'Winters of December,
come and take this heart away
Come and take this heart to that page, of that book, where I
first met her, come, and take me there.
Come, and take me there, where it all started.
Where it all, will end.
Take me there.'

Sanoj Joseph

Just a simple guy, living off simple things.

Remedy

"Come with me," a smile across your face,
While taking my hand and running across the field,
It was a whole lot of green,
And a lot of blue tulips spread across.
I never knew this place, so it was surprising,
Or was I startled?
Was this place unknown,
Or was it her warmth, familiar but strange,
Or maybe it was the closeness that made me feel so,
But I knew that here was the most tranquil I had ever felt.
"Where are you taking me, hun?"
It wasn't surprising that there was only silence,
Sure there were giggles and a whole lot of excitement.
What was I expecting, a reply?
Girls, when they are determined, they just wanna lead.
Isn't it worth it? I know the answer..
I do it almost all the time, so lost in thoughts,
Just looking at her, enthralled by all that she is,
So, I had not known that we had stopped running.
It was a hard kick on the back of my knee,
That brought me back to this world,
I could see her fake frowns when she said,
"Man, not again!"
She laid on the green grass, while motioning me to do so,
A really big smile on her, " let's see some meteor showers".
I smiled, too, while laying on the ground next to her.
'Man, look!" She pointed to the sky, all excited,
A lot of bright streaks racing across the darkness spread above,
Like nature's fireworks!
It sure was beautiful, she was, too, maybe even more.
No, surely more. Much, much more!

She took my hand, crossing fingers with hers,
And then kept it on her stomach,
The warmth I felt,
I wasn't sure what I was excited about,
Cos it was a warmth unlike anything that I had ever known,
This space between us,
Maybe this is what home feels like,
I was happy, too.
She looked at me and said, it's beautiful, no?
Yes, you're beautiful! I said, so lost in her eyes.
"Oh please, let's look at the stars now," she said to me,
"Oh sweet thing, Oh my favourite human being ever,
You, you are the only star that I ever want to see,
Shining so damn bright, and bringing light to my life,"
I said to her..
"Close your eyes." She said,
"You won't be here when I wake up,
and I'll find myself in that dark place,
You dragged me away from, if I do that,
So let me linger by you till the last second,
cos by your side is where I'm enough."
I gave her the blue tulip that I had gotten from the way,
And said to her, "Sweetheart, be my remedy.."
"I will be... your remedy" she said, smiling...

Sara Srivastava

Sara Srivastava is a student from grade 10 from New Delhi, India.

A science aficionado and a literature connoisseur, Sara has a deeply felt love for writing and a thirst for bringing impactful change in the world. A poet and blogger who likes to conjure up dreamscapes, she considers poetry to be her tether to this world, and her ship to steer in the waters of the unknown.

For her, writing is a way to tell your story, in a world where people hardly listen and words are the one constant, whether it is grief, anger or happiness. Our lives too, are a story to someone else, and she believes it's a beautiful legacy to leave behind.

Their Own

Met in rare dreams, in a raindrop that fell from the heavens.
Both craved for the voices to echo their names.

Cascaded like a ship, wrecked in tumultuous waters.
Both wanted it to be etched in their fables, when sunken deep and buried.

Brew a storm that whisked one away, left alone the other.
Both yearned, a race to the stars, but only with one another.

The other waited for the one, as faithful as the tide of the moonlight.
Both leapt into the colours of one another as the skies glimmered of something, something worthwhile.

The one saw the other battered and bruised by all that was ever loved.
Both befallen to a tragic tale, where the stars belonged to the one, but not the other.

The seas, the heavens, the stars, mere meaningless words remained.
Both found one another, as true as the whispers on a child.

Aeons and lifetimes of whites and blues, silvers and reds, blacks and greens.
Both painted a universe so divine, unheard were any voices but theirs, unseen were any stars so bewitching, their homeric storm dappled with peace, bound together by faith,
And a world, their own.

Simran Dumra

Words are the most inexhaustible source of magic, words can make you or break you, they are powerful. Simran loves words whether they be in books or poems or songs, and after many years of devouring words, she decided to use them to write poems of her own.

Loving someone

Loving someone is painful
Because they don't treat your heart well
And tear it to pieces
Loving someone is painful
Because at times
they don't love you back
Loving someone is painful
Because sometimes you have to watch them fall apart
In front of your eyes, and it hurts
But you can't do anything to help
Loving someone is painful
Because they don't believe you
And you don't know what else to do
To prove to them that you do love them
Loving someone is painful
Because they don't trust you
Even when you would trust them with your life
Loving someone is painful
Because you give all of yourself
And don't get anything in return
Loving someone is painful
Because you hate them but you also love them
Because you want to scream at them but you also want to
hear their laughter
Loving someone is painful
I know all that already
I have been through it enough times
So why is it that I still love you?
Loving someone is painful

But why does the pain seem worth it
when it comes to you
Loving someone is painful
So why am I ready to let my heart
Be ripped to shreds if it is by your hands?

Loving someone is painful
So why am I am ready to love you
Till the day I die?
Loving someone is painful
So why am I ready to hold you through
All the bad phases and all the hurricanes?
Loving someone is painful
So why am I ready to remind you every time
That I do love you despite everything?
Loving someone is painful
So why am I willing to wait till you finally trust me
And let me in?
Loving someone is painful
So why am I ready to give all of me
Even if you give nothing back
Loving you is painful
And yet I can't stop.

Sonali Mondal

Writer & Book Lover

A Girl

Yes, I am a Girl
Feel like a pearl;
I want to touch the sky,
My dreams are very high.
Yes, I am precious;
Like my Jesus.
Please don't stop my way,
My dreams are not away.
I want to overcome all
the obstacles of life;
Want to live the life,
Like a melody of fife.

Sudhandira Sahana Arumugam

A human, a writer, a budding doc. Too young by heart, too old by soul, too much of paradox to ever correctly describe.

'tis the damn season

It was the spring after seven winters,
the greens and blossoms so radiant
that it hurt the parched eyes.
You and me, kids by the river
were plucking dandelions and chasing butterflies,
like the winter never even existed.

It was a spring like never before, they said -
a spring
that thawed every bit of lurking coldness.
'Tis the damn season, they said -
a season
that welcomed happiness like a twin sister.
You and me, chances and glances,
were fireflies dancing under the moonlight,
wrapped in the promise of sunrise.
Oh, little did we know,
forever is an artifice contrived by ignorance.

The spring stretched beyond the horizon,
with showers that brought life,
and joy seasoned with contention.
You and me, pauses and progress
were a pair of snowdrops reveling in the warmth.
Oh, little did we know,
we were also waiting it out.

The spring gave flowers for a century, they said.
No wonder we got carried away by roses
and didn't heed the thorns.
'Tis the damn season, they said.

No wonder it had so much of heaven
to sugar-coat an apocalypse.
You and me, silence and nonchalance,
were lost stars drifting apart
as the autumn rolled in.

It was the spring after seven winters
and it came undone with glittery confetti,
smelling like childhood.
You and me,
either not good enough to last
or just too good to last,
were the farewell lullaby of a season
that not only lived
but also departed with grace.

Tanishka Soni

Tanishka, a student as well as a teacher, is a girl who seeks perfection in every sphere of life. She settles in nothing less than success. She has been adoring, admiring and writing poetries and other art forms since her teenage. Tanishka aspires to publish her own novel someday. She loves to listen to stories of different people because she believes that every human has something new and unique to share!

Pain is Strength

I inscribed your name yet again,
"Daddy", the word said, depicting my pain!
With a heart that misses, and the memories that bother,
I asked, "Why is it that you left me, father?"
You told me you would be back someday soon,
But it has been years that you went up with the moon!
You advised me to be firm and strong,
But why did you not tell me of the ways to face the wrong?
I was your princess, and no one could tolerate,
So they filled me with coldness and all the hate!
You have been my savior all this while,
Giving me strength to hide tears and smile!
You taught me to keep promises,
But, who except you will fulfill my wishes?
When midnight strikes and I talk to you in ways unknown,
I remember the tie that binds us, too sacred to be shown!
You are my secret, I keep away from this world,
Even when you are a distant memory where everything's blurred.
Don't tell nobody that we converse at times,
Let people believe that your girl's fine!
For, "Pain is Strength" were your sayings,
And ever since I've tried all the darings!
You promised to bring heaven at my feet,
But you broke the vow, why'd you cheat?
You said forever but left so soon,
I miss you daddy, every night and noon!

Unnati Goyal

Unnati is a management geek, poet by heart, and student of life.

She began writing like many others, as her escape from the monotony of physics and chemistry in the dull classrooms. With no desire to be tied down by a Romeo, she found the freedom she craved between the pages of books and ink of her pen. She dreams to give others the inspiration for their love letters.

To the one who tied my soul with Conundrum

You took the part of me
Like the bee soaks the nectar of flower,
You made me gloomy
Like children who abandoned their parents,
You tied me with your remembrance
Like an adult who has memories of childhood,
You left me with caginess
Like a wine left in the glass,
I wonder if I'll get my love in future
Or someone will again leave me with mental torture.

Vanshika Jingar

Vanshika is an Assistant Professor at Parul University, Vadodara. She is also doing PhD in Civil (Geotechnical Engineering). She is always ready to be involved in co-curricular activities. In addition to teaching and studying she is also interested in writing poems, playing keyboard and other extra curricular activities.

मेरा वॉरियर बच्चा

(Poetry is regarding the unborn child. It is the poem of a mother who faces miscarriage.)

वो दिन याद है,
जब तेरे आने की खबर मिली थी,
खुश थी बहुत, के मेरी जान में एक रूह बसी थी

बहुत ज्यादा सोचती थी,
खुद के लिए कम,
तेरे लिए ज्यादा,
खुद के लिए शून्य
तेरे लिए अगणित से भी ज्यादा,
बहुत खुश रह रही थी में,
खुद के लिए कम,
तेरे लिए हर बार ज्यादा ।।

छोड़ दी थी शेरो शायरी हमने,
क्यूंकि शायद गम में नहीं थी,
लिख नही पाते थे,
फिर भी हम खुश थे,

आज पूरी किताब भी लिख दी,
फिर भी हम खुश नही थे,
काहनी पूरी होने पे भी खुशी मे नही थे ।।

तू मैरी हर तकलीफ में रहे लिया,
खा पी के मस्त जी लिया
मेरा वॉरियर बच्चा,
हर जंग जीत लिया
सब सह के भी खुश रह लिया ।।

पता नही कहा में चूक गई,
के तूने मुझे छोड़ दिया,
जब साथ था तभी मुझे बदल दिया,
जाते जाते तो पूरी जिंदगी बदल गया,

दुआ हे मेरी,
जहा जाए वहा खुश रहे,
बिना देखे,
इश्क करना सीखा जाए,
कुछ भी हो जाए,
मेरा वॉरियर बच्चा,
हर बार तू जीत जाए ।।।

Vinita Singh

Vinita has done master of law from Deen Dayal Upadhyay Gorakhpur University. She grew up in Gorakhpur(Uttar Pradesh). Obsessed with books since kindergarten, she loves to read Literature, and also write. Her first book is a fantasy Novel 'Niyati' .

ये शहर, वो शहर तो नहीं

ये शहर,वो शहर तो नहीं
जिससे हम थे रुख़सत हुए।
ये शहर वो शहर तो नहीं
जिसके हर पल को हम थे जिए।
ये शहर वो शहर तो नहीं
जहाँ अनगिनत लम्हें हमने संजोए थे।
ये शहर वो शहर तो नहीं
जिनके गालियो में फक्कर से घुमा करते थे।
बदल गयी तेरी भी आबो हवा ऐ शहर
ओढ़ लिया तुमने भी रोशनी की चादर ।
मशगूल है तू भी बाजार की भीड़ में ऐ शहर
जहाँ सुकून के लम्हें बांटा करते थे।
ये शहर वो शहर तो नहीं
जिसके हर फिज़ा से हम थे रुबरु हुए।
ये शहर वो शहर तो नहीं
कुछ अजनबी से जहाँ हम लगने लगे।
ये शहर वो शहर तो नहीं
जिससे हम थे रुख़सत हुए।

Yadhu Krishna Menon

You can usually find Yadhu with a cup of coffee and his head buried in any one of Dan Brown's classics or trying to make sense out of Rumi's poetries. He's always had a passion for writing and that has spilled on over to his Instagram page where you can see his works put out for the world to see. A content writer by profession, Yadhu finds joy in traveling every now and then and also in screaming his lungs out when Bayern Munich wins a match.

The Brook

A brook now separates us,
No rocks lay on the surface,
Nor do any plants grow on it.
I stand on the bank,
My eyes weary and head heavy,
I try to think,
But my thoughts don't form,
Nor do words escape my mouth.
Unaware and dazed,
My gaze falls on the other side.
There you stand,
Strong and with your head high,
Your eyes look straight,
A piercing look,
Staring into my soul,
Tearing into my heart,
But the light that once shone no longer lingers,
And the warmth that you radiated no longer whispers,
No lush forests,
Or hidden canopies outline your bank,
No sandy shores,
Or cedar trees stand for you to lean on,
You stand on gravel strewn with bones,
And sleep on floors drenched with blood,
Monsters haunt your dreams,
And demons shred your skin,
And yet you stand,
Looking straight.

A brook now separates us,
No rocks lay on the surface,
Nor do any plants grow on it.
I stand on the bank,
With blank eyes and a numb mind,
I stare forward,
Unknowingly and unwillingly,
My gaze falls on the other side.
There you stand,
With a fool's face and a wide yawn,
Your eyes look straight,
A prying look,
Glancing into my veins,
Peering into my chains,
But your eyes no longer seek,
And your heart now lays bleak,
No tall buildings,
Or busy pavements outline your bank,
No cozy balconies,
Or towering posts stand for you to lean on,
You stand on concrete covered with filth,
And sleep on beds draped with hatred,
Fiends chase you while you sleep,
And ghouls whisper from your shadows,
And yet you stand,
Looking straight.

Our shores are empty,
And our hands are filthy.
We trudge over to the bank,
Our stares locked,
We desperately want to cross over,
But we can't,
Our words are not heard,

And our voices are lost,
All we can do is stare,
And wonder what might have been,
But the brook never abandons,
And the brook never forgets,
The brook reflects,
And curiosity triumphs,
We break our gaze,
And we stare,
Stare into our reflections,
But we see not ourselves,
Rather each other,
A face with a wide smile,
A ball of happiness,
Taking me on a ride,
Showing me life.
A face with a bright grin,
An ocean of patience,
Holding you hard,
Showing you love.
Our images are our strength,
Our beliefs are our power,
The brook may separate us now,
But soon we'll jump,
And together we'll swim,
Swim across oceans,
Swim past trenches,
Swim towards a new horizon.

Yash Singhal

Corporate by profession, poet by nature, Yash is a graduate from IIT Bombay who loves adventures. In a bid to express his emotions better, he took the help of poetry. This piece is a reminisce of his life in Mumbai and in some sense is a depiction of his emotional attachment to the city. With this he hopes to strike a cord with every person who has experienced the beautiful life of this beautiful city.

Mumbai

Afternoon's blazing sun and the bustling traffic run,
The shining lights at night, people everywhere in sight.
I don't know what makes it truly alive,
But somehow everything in this city is right.

Every soul has something to do, somewhere to be,
Rushing into the day, stuffed in trains so tight.
Never stopping for anything but the red light,
Still somehow everything in this city is right.

The rains flood the street, 6 months at a time,
Jammed are the roads, with no respite.
Yet none gives a damn, no distress no fight,
Somehow everything in this city is alright.

Hopes are destroyed and shattered every day,
Yet everyone begins the day fresh and bright.
A new creed of dreamers awake every night,
How is everything in this city always so right?

This is a deep hole, but an escape in its own right,
Man, I wonder how everything in Mumbai is always so right?